Instant PhoneGap Social App Development

Consume social network feeds and share social network content using native plugins and PhoneGap

Kerri Shotts

BIRMINGHAM - MUMBAI

Instant PhoneGap Social App Development

First published: January 2013

Production Reference: 1210113

Published by Packt Publishing Ltd.
Livery Place
35 Livery Street
Birmingham B3 2PB, UK.

ISBN 978-1-84969-628-9

www.packtpub.com

Credits

Author
Kerri Shotts

Reviewers
Becky Gibson

Julio César Sánchez

Acquisition Editor
Dilip Venkatesh

Commissioning Editor
Ameya Sawant

Technical Editor
Nitee Shetty

Project Coordinator
Amigya Khurana

Proofreader
Aaron Nash

Graphics
Aditi Gajjar

Production Coordinators
Aparna Bhagat

Nitesh Thakur

Cover Work
Aparna Bhagat

Cover Image
Aditi Gajjar

About the Author

Kerri Shotts has been programming since she learned BASIC on her Commodore 64. She earned her degree in Computer Science and has worked as a Test Engineer and Database Administrator. Now a Technology Consultant, she helps her clients with custom websites, apps (desktop and mobile), and more. When not at the computer, she enjoys photography and taking care of her aquariums.

About the Reviewers

Becky Gibson is a senior technical staff member in IBM's Emerging Internet Technologies Group. Her current focus is contributing to the open source Apache Cordova (PhoneGap) project to enable building compelling mobile applications using Web technologies. She was the Accessibility Lead for the Dojo Open Source JavaScript Toolkit and was responsible for implementing full accessibility in the core widget set. She participated in the development of the W3C WAI-ARIA (Accessible Rich Internet Applications) specification and was a contributor in the W3C Web Content Accessibility Guidelines Working Group for several years. She continues her commitment to accessibility by implementing it in iOS features in Cordova and promoting mobile accessibility.

She has over 20 years of development experience in languages ranging from PC assembly, C, C++, Java, Objective-C, to web technologies. She has contributed to various Lotus and IBM projects including Lotus 1-2-3 and IBM Lotus Notes. She has a BS degree from the University of Maine and an MS in Computer Science from Boston University.

Julio César Sánchez has been a professional software developer since 2007. Over the years he has worked with many different technologies, most of them being web related. In 2010, he discovered PhoneGap and he has been following the PhoneGap Google group since then, learning, helping other developers, and even contributing with a PhoneGap plugin. He spends some of his spare time developing mobile apps. You can visit his Web to get to know more about him and his work at `www.solucionesmovil.es`.

www.PacktPub.com

Support files, eBooks, discount offers and more

You might want to visit www.PacktPub.com for support files and downloads related to your book.

Did you know that Packt offers eBook versions of every book published, with PDF and ePub files available? You can upgrade to the eBook version at www.PacktPub.com and as a print book customer, you are entitled to a discount on the eBook copy. Get in touch with us at service@packtpub.com for more details.

At www.PacktPub.com, you can also read a collection of free technical articles, sign up for a range of free newsletters and receive exclusive discounts and offers on Packt books and eBooks.

http://PacktLib.PacktPub.com

Do you need instant solutions to your IT questions? PacktLib is Packt's online digital book library. Here, you can access, read and search across Packt's entire library of books.

Why Subscribe?

- ▶ Fully searchable across every book published by Packt
- ▶ Copy and paste, print and bookmark content
- ▶ On demand and accessible via web browser

Free Access for Packt account holders

If you have an account with Packt at www.PacktPub.com, you can use this to access PacktLib today and view nine entirely free books. Simply use your login credentials for immediate access.

Table of Contents

Preface

Instant PhoneGap Social App Development shows you how to create compelling mobile apps that integrate with social media based on PhoneGap/Cordova. This book will show you how to consume Twitter feeds and also how to share content to Twitter using Twitter Web Intents.

What this book covers

What do we build? introduces us to the app that we will be building in this book using Twitter streams and Twitter Web Intents.

Creating the project focuses on preparing the project by downloading all the necessary components and creating the appropriate directory structure.

Designing the UI/interaction describes how we can design our user interface and also covers the interaction between the various widgets and views.

Designing the data model covers the task where we design our data model for handling Twitter users and streams.

Implementing the data model describes the implementation of our data model and creation of five Twitter accounts that we will use. We will also be introduced to the loadJSON method in PKUTIL and the Twitter API.

Configuring the ChildBrowser plugin covers the installation and configuration of the ChildBrowser plugin.

Implementing the start view describes the creation of our first view in our app, the start view. It outlines the basic view as well as helps us explore with the complementary functions of the view.

Implementing the social view explains the creation of the social view where we will display our Twitter stream. We also explore how we can use the Twitter stream data to construct a Twitter stream that the end user can interact with.

Implementing the tweet view introduces the last view, the tweet view, where the user interacts with a given tweet. We also see how this view gives the user the opportunity to share the tweet via Twitter Web Intents.

Putting it all together outlines the creation of the app.js file and two HTML files under the www directory to get a fully functional app on our hands so that we can load the app and start it off.

What you need for this book

The example application in this book is based on PhoneGap/Cordova 2.2. If you download a more recent version, be sure to replace the cordova-2.2.0-ios.js and cordova-2.2.0-android.js references with the appropriate versions.

To build/run the code supplied for the book, the following software is required (divided by platform where appropriate):

	Windows	Linux	OS X
For iOS Apps			
IDE			XCode 4.5+
OS			OS X 10.7+
SDK			iOS 5+
For Android Apps			
IDE	Eclipse 4.x Classic	Eclipse 4.x Classic	Eclipse 4.x Classic
OS	XP or newer	Any modern distro supporting Eclipse & Android SDK – Ubuntu, RHEL, etc.	OS X 10.6+ (probably works on lower versions)
Java	1.6 or higher	1.6 or higher	1.6 or higher
SDK	Version 15+	Version 15+	Version 15+
For All Platforms			
Apache Cordova / PhoneGap	2.2	2.2	2.2
Plugins	Current	Current	Current

Some useful websites that can be used for software download are as follows:

- Xcode at https://developer.apple.com/xcode/
- iOS SDK at https://developer.apple.com/devcenter/ios/index.action
- Eclipse at http://www.eclipse.org/downloads/packages/eclipse-classic-421/junosr1

- ▶ Android SDK at `http://developer.android.com/sdk/index.html`
- ▶ Apache Cordova/PhoneGap at `http://phonegap.com/download`
- ▶ Plugins at `https://github.com/phonegap/phonegap-plugins`

Who this book is for

You'll need to have a desire to learn about mobile application development. Since PhoneGap uses HTML, CSS, and Javascript heavily, it is important to have a good understanding of these topics. You should also have a good understanding of your desired platform and corresponding SDK and IDE. (That is, if you want to develop for Android, you should be familiar with Eclipse. For iOS, you need to be familiar with Xcode).

Conventions

In this book, you will find a number of styles of text that distinguish between different kinds of information. Here are some examples of these styles, and an explanation of their meaning.

Code words in text are shown as follows: "The `getScreenName()` method simply returns the screen name."

A block of code is set as follows:

```
self.getScreenName = function ()
  {
    return self._screenName;
  }
```

When we wish to draw your attention to a particular part of a code block, the relevant lines or items are set in bold:

```
function (success)
  {
    if (success)
      {
        startView.initializeView();
        PKUI.CORE.showView (startView);
      }
  });
```

Any command-line input or output is written as follows:

```
# cp /usr/src/asterisk-addons/configs/cdr_mysql.conf.sample
    /etc/asterisk/cdr_mysql.conf
```

New terms and **important words** are shown in bold. Words that you see on the screen, in menus or dialog boxes for example, appear in the text like this: " Click on **Next >**".

> Warnings or important notes appear in a box like this.

> Tips and tricks appear like this.

Reader feedback

Feedback from our readers is always welcome. Let us know what you think about this book—what you liked or may have disliked. Reader feedback is important for us to develop titles that you really get the most out of.

To send us general feedback, simply send an e-mail to feedback@packtpub.com, and mention the book title via the subject of your message.

If there is a book that you need and would like to see us publish, please send us a note in the **SUGGEST A TITLE** form on www.packtpub.com or e-mail suggest@packtpub.com.

If there is a topic that you have expertise in and you are interested in either writing or contributing to a book, see our author guide on www.packtpub.com/authors.

Customer support

Now that you are the proud owner of a Packt book, we have a number of things to help you to get the most from your purchase.

Downloading the example code

You can download the example code files for all Packt books you have purchased from your account at http://www.PacktPub.com. If you purchased this book elsewhere, you can visit http://www.PacktPub.com/support and register to have the files e-mailed directly to you.

Errata

Although we have taken every care to ensure the accuracy of our content, mistakes do happen. If you find a mistake in one of our books—maybe a mistake in the text or the code—we would be grateful if you would report this to us. By doing so, you can save other readers from frustration and help us improve subsequent versions of this book. If you find any errata, please report them by visiting http://www.packtpub.com/support, selecting your book, clicking on the **errata submission form** link, and entering the details of your errata. Once your errata are verified, your submission will be accepted and the errata will be uploaded on our website, or added to any list of existing errata, under the Errata section of that title. Any existing errata can be viewed by selecting your title from http://www.packtpub.com/support.

Piracy

Piracy of copyright material on the Internet is an ongoing problem across all media. At Packt, we take the protection of our copyright and licenses very seriously. If you come across any illegal copies of our works, in any form, on the Internet, please provide us with the location address or website name immediately so that we can pursue a remedy.

Please contact us at copyright@packtpub.com with a link to the suspected pirated material.

We appreciate your help in protecting our authors, and our ability to bring you valuable content.

Questions

You can contact us at questions@packtpub.com if you are having a problem with any aspect of the book, and we will do our best to address it.

Instant PhoneGap Social App Development

Welcome to PhoneGap social app development. Social networking has changed the way we share information in our world. Where it used to be an e-mail to a friend (or even a letter!), now it's a tweet or a Facebook post, often for the world to see. What's even more amazing is how relatively young the various social networks are and how quickly they have changed the way we communicate and consume information. Because of this transformation, our apps need to support sharing to social networks, lest our app appear dated.

 You'll often see the word `Cordova` in our code examples in this book. PhoneGap was recently acquired by Adobe and the underlying code was given to the Apache Incubator project. This project is named `Cordova`, and PhoneGap utilizes it to provide its various services. So if you see `Cordova`, it really means the same thing for now.

What do we build?

In this section, we will build an app that illustrates both sides of the social network equation. The first is that of consuming information from various sources – we'll be using Twitter streams for this. The second is that of sharing information – we'll be using Twitter's Web Intents to accomplish this. You can find more information about Twitter Web Intents at `https://dev.twitter.com/docs/intents`.

 One can use each platform's native sharing capabilities, and this will be a challenge at the end of this chapter. For some platforms, sharing is easy, while on an iOS in particular, it's downright painful – thus the choice to go with Twitter Web Intents.

What does it do?

Our app, called Socializer, will display the Twitter streams from five pre-set Twitter accounts. The user can then read these streams, and should they find an interesting tweet, they can tap on it to do more with it. For example, they may wish to view a link embedded in the tweet. More importantly, the end user may wish to share the information using Twitter, and the app will offer a **Share** button to do just that.

To accomplish this, we'll be working with Twitter's **JSON API**, a natural fit for an app already written largely in JavaScript. The only downside is that Twitter has a pretty low cap for rate-limiting API requests, so we'll also have to build some basic support for when this occurs. (For more information about rate-limiting, see `https://dev.twitter.com/docs/rate-limiting`.) To be honest, this is far more likely to occur to us as a developer than the user, because we often reload the app to test a new feature, which incurs new API requests far faster than an end user would typically incur them.

We'll also introduce the concept of PhoneGap plugins, as we'll be using the ChildBrowser plugin, which is supported across both iOS and Android, and opens web content within the app, rather than outside the app. This is important, since once the user is outside the app, they may not return to the app.

Why is it great?

This project is a great introduction to handling APIs using JSON, including Twitter's API. While we're using a very small subset of Twitter's API, the lessons learned in this project can be expanded to deal with the rest of the API. Furthermore, JSON APIs are all over the place, and learning how to deal with Twitter's API is a great way to learn how to deal with any JSON API.

We'll also be dealing with how to share content. To do this, we'll work with Twitter's Web Intents, a convenient and extremely simple method that allows sharing of content without messing with the account information or complicated code.

We'll also be working with PhoneGap plugins, which many apps will eventually require in one way or another. For example, our app should be able to handle links to external websites – the best way to do this is to have the ChildBrowser plugin handle it. This lets the user stay inside our app and easily return to our app when they are done. Without it, we'd be taking the user out of the app and into the default browser.

The app itself will also serve to introduce you to creating mobile apps using a simple framework named **YASMF** (**Yet Another Simple, Mobile Framework**). There are a multitude of fantastic frameworks out there (jQuery Mobile, jQuery Touch, iUI, Sencha Touch, and so on.), and the framework you choose to use ultimately doesn't really matter that much—they all do what they advertise—and our using a custom framework isn't intended to throw you off-kilter in any fashion. The main reason for using this particular custom framework is that it's very lightweight and simple; which means the concepts it uses will be easy to transfer to any framework. For more information regarding the framework, please visit `https://github.com/photokandyStudios/YASMF/wiki`.

How are we going to do it?

To do this, we're going to break down the creation of our app into several different parts. We'll be focusing on the design of the app before we handle the implementation using the following:

- ▶ Creating the project
- ▶ Designing the UI/interaction
- ▶ Designing the data model
- ▶ Implementing the data model
- ▶ Configuring the ChildBrowser plugin
- ▶ Implementing the start view
- ▶ Implementing the social view
- ▶ Implementing the tweet view
- ▶ Putting it all together

Creating the project

Before we can create the app, we need to prepare for the project by downloading all the necessary components (PhoneGap, YASMF, and so on) and create the appropriate directory structure.

How to do it...

1. Download the latest version of PhoneGap from `http://phonegap.com/download`, currently 2.2.0 at the time of writing, and extract it to the appropriate directory. (For example, I use `/Applications/phonegap/phonegap220`.) Make sure that you have also installed the appropriate IDEs (Xcode for iOS development, and Eclipse for Android development).

2. Next, download the latest version of the YASMF framework from `https://github.com/photokandyStudios/YASMF/downloads`, and extract it anywhere. (For example, I used my `Downloads` folder.)

3. You'll also need to download the PhoneGap plugins repository available at `http://www.github.com/phonegap/phonegap-plugins`. This will ensure you have all the necessary plugins we'll need as well as any plugins you might be interested in working with on your own.

Downloading the example code

You can download the example code files for all Packt books you have purchased from your account at `http://www.PacktPub.com`. If you purchased this book elsewhere, you can visit `http://www.PacktPub.com/support` and register to have the files e-mailed directly to you.

4. Next, you need to create a project for the various platforms you intend to support. Here's how we create both projects at once on Mac OS X. The commands should translate to Linux and Android-only projects with a little modification, and the same should apply to creating Android projects on Windows with some additional modifications. For the following steps, consider `$PROJECT_HOME` to be the location of your project, `$PHONEGAP_HOME` to be the location where you installed PhoneGap, and `$YASMF_DOWNLOAD` to be the location where you extracted the YASMF framework. The code snippet is as follows:

```
mkdir $PROJECT_HOME
cd $PROJECT_HOME
mkdir Android iOS www
cd $PHONEGAP_HOME/lib/android/bin
./create $PROJECT_HOME/Android/Socializer com.yourcompany.
Socializer Socializer
cd $PHONEGAP_HOME/lib/ios/bin
./create $PROJECT_HOME/iOS com.yourcompany.Socializer
Socializer
cd $PROJECT_HOME
mkdir www/cordova
cp Android/Socializer/assets/www/cordova-2.2.0.js www/cordova/
cordova-2.2.0-android.js
cp iOS/www/cordova-2.2.0.js www/cordova/cordova-2.2.0-ios.js
cd Android/Socializer/assets
rm -rf www
ln -s ../../../www
cd ../../../iOS
rm -rf www
```

```
ln   -s ../www
cd ..
cd www
cp -r $YASMF_DOWNLOAD/framework .
mkdir images models views style childbrowser plugins
cd plugins
mkdir Android iOS
cd ../..
cd Android/Socializer/src/com/phonegaphotshot/Socializer
```

5. Edit `Socializer.java`.

6. Change `index.html` to `index_android.html`. (This points the Android version at the correct index file.)

7. Save the file using the following code line:

    ```
    cd $PROJECT_HOME/iOS/Socializer
    ```

8. Edit `Cordova.plist`.

9. Search for `UIWebViewBounce`.

10. Change the `<true/>` tag just below `UIWebViewBounce` to `<false/>`. (This ensures that the WebView itself can't scroll, something that should never happen in an iOS app, otherwise the user will be able to tell that the app isn't native.)

11. Search for `ShowSplashScreenSpinner`.

12. Change the `<true/>` just below `ShowSplashScreenSpinner` to `<false/>`. (This ensures that the WebView itself can't scroll, something that should never happen in an iOS app, otherwise the user will be able to tell that the app isn't native.)

13. Search for `ExternalHosts`.

14. Remove the `<array/>` tag and replace it with "`<array>`", "`<string>*</string>`", "`</array>`". This isn't always something that you would want to do for a production app, but as it allows for our apps to access the Internet with no restrictions, it's good for testing purposes.

15. Save the file.

16. Edit `Socializer-info.plist`.

17. Above the line containing `UISupportedInterfaceOrientations`, add "`<key>UIStatusBarStyle</key>`", "`<string>UIStatusBarStyleBlackOpaq ue</string>`". (This makes the iOS app have a black status bar.)

18. Start Eclipse.

19. Navigate to **File | New | Project....**

20. Select **Android Project**.

21. Click on **Next >**.

22. Select the **Create project from existing source** option.

23. Click on the **Browse** icon.

24. Navigate to `$PROJECT_HOME/Android/Socializer/`.

25. Click on **Open**.

26. Click on **Next >**.

27. Uncheck and re-check the highest **Google APIs** entry. (For some reason, Eclipse doesn't always keep the correct SDK version when doing this, so you may have to go back after the project is created and reset it. Just right-click on any directory, **Configure Build Paths...** and go to the **Android** section. Then you can re-select the highest SDK.)

28. Click on **Next >**.

29. Change the **Minimum SDK** level to 8.

30. Click on **Finish**.

31. Start Xcode.

32. Navigate to **File | Open...**.

33. Navigate to the project in `$PROJECT_HOME/iOS`.

34. Click on **Open**.

35. At this point you should have Xcode and Eclipse open with the project. Close both; we'll be using our favorite editor for now.

The project thus created results in the following directory structure:

- `/Android`: The Android project
- `/iOS`: The iOS project
- `/www`

  - `/cordova`: We'll place the PhoneGap support libraries here
  - `/framework`: Our framework will be in this directory
  - `/cultures`: Any localization configuration will be placed in this framework, which comes with `en-US`
  - `/images`: All of our images will be in this directory
  - `/views`: All of our views will be in this directory
  - `/models`: All of our data models will be in this directory
  - `/style`: Any custom CSS we need to use will be in this directory

- ❏ /childbrowser: Android-specific assets for ChildBrowser will be in this directory
- ❏ /plugins: Plugins should go in this directory
- ❏ /Android: Android-specific plugins are in this directory
- ❏ /iOS: iOS-specific plugins are in this directory

Designing the UI/interaction

Our first task is to design our user interface and the interaction between the various widgets and views. Like the previous task, we will have three views: the *start* view, the *social* view, and the *tweet* view.

How to do it...

We'll begin with the start view. This will be a very simple view. It is entirely optional in this app as all we'll be doing is explaining the app and providing a way to move to the main view.

With that in mind, our sketch is shown in the following screenshot:

In the preceding image, we have a **Start** button (1) that will push the social view onto the view stack. We also have some explanatory text (2).

Our next view is the social view shown in the following screenshot:

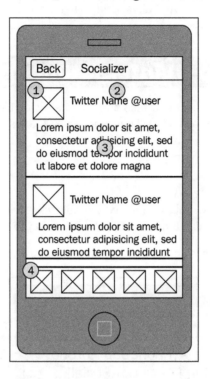

The social view is essentially a list of tweets, one after the other. We'll display several tweets at a time, and as such, we'll have to deal with scrolling at some point. While you can use various libraries to accomplish this, we'll be using our own minimalist scrolling library.

Each tweet will consist of a profile image (1), the screen name and real name (if available) (2), and the text of the tweet (3). When the user taps a tweet, we'll transition to the tweet view.

At the bottom of the view (4), we have a series of profile images for five different Twitter accounts. The images will be retrieved from Twitter itself; we won't be storing the images ourselves. When an image is tapped, we'll load the respective Twitter stream.

Our tweet view looks like the following screenshot:

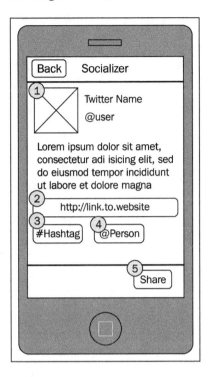

First, note that our tweet view repeats the tweet (1) that the user tapped on in the social view. The same information is repeated, but we also list the various web links (2) that the tweets might have, any hashtags (3), and any user mentions (4). Items (2) to (4) are intended to be tappable, that is, if a user taps on (2), they should be taken to the particular website. If they tap on (3), they should be taken back to the social view with a stream of tweets referencing the hashtag. The same should happen if they tap on (4), except that it would be that particular user's stream.

We also have a **Back** button in our navigation bar to takes the user back to the previous view, and a **Share** button (5) in our toolbar, when tapped, should display the ChildBrowser plugin with the Twitter Web Intent already displayed. If the user isn't logged in to Twitter, they'll be prompted to do so. Once logged in, they'll be given the tweet (which they can change to suit their needs), and they can then send it out to their followers. When complete, the user can close the ChildBrowser plugin and return to the app.

Now that we created our mockup, we need to define some of the resources we'll need. Let's open up our editing program and get busy designing our app.

The following screenshot is a pretty good representation of how our final product will look:

A lot of this can be accomplished using CSS. The background of the Twitter stream and the navigation bar are the only two components that will be difficult, so we should save those out to our www/images directory as Background.png and NavigationBar.png respectively. If you notice, both have a texture, so make sure to save them in a way that they will tile without visible seams.

For this task, we've defined how our UI should look, and the various interactions between widgets and views. We also generated a mockup of the app in our graphics editor and created some image resources for later use.

Designing the data model

In this task, we will design our data model for handling Twitter users and streams. Our model will, to some extent, rely on Twitter's model as well as the results that it returns from its API we will use unmodified. We will be defining the rest of the model in this task.

How to do it...

Let's take a look at our data model:

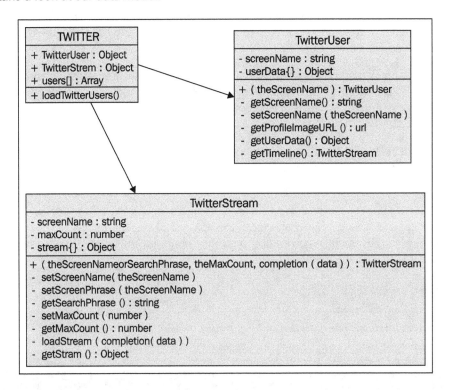

We'll be using TWITTER as the namespace and within it, we'll have two objects that we'll be using a lot: TwitterUser and TwitterStream. The idea behind TwitterUser is to be an instance of a particular user, which we'll be representing with an image on the toolbar in the streams view. The TwitterStream object will be a representation of a single stream.

Let's examine TwitterUser more closely. The object has two properties, screenName and userData. screenName holds the user's Twitter username. userData will hold the response from Twitter's API. It will have lots of different information about the user, including their profile image URL, their real name, and more.

The constructor will return an initialized TwitterUser based upon the supplied screen name. Internally, the constructor just calls the setScreenName() method which will request the user data from Twitter. The getScreenName() method simply returns the screen name. The getProfileImageUrl() method will return the URL to the user's profile image. The getUserData() will return the data that Twitter returned, and the getTimeline() method will create a TwitterStream object for the particular user.

The `TwitterStream` object operates on a similar idea: it will house the data returned by Twitter. The `TwitterStream` object also provides us the ability to get a stream for a particular user as well as the ability to return a stream for any search (such as a hashtag).

When constructed, we pass three options, the screen name or the search phrase, the maximum number of tweets to return (up to 200), and a function to call when the stream has finished loading.

The `loadStream()` method does the actual work of loading a Twitter stream based on the above options passed to the object when created. It gets called immediately upon construction of the object so that our app doesn't have to send a separate message asking for the stream to be loaded.

Some methods related to the properties in the object that we have are `setScreenName()`, `setSearchPhrase()`, `getSearchPhrase()`, `setMaxCount()`, `getMaxCount()` and `getStream()`.

The `setScreenName()` method does the same thing as setting the `searchPhrase()` method except that it adds an @ character to the name. The `loadStream()` method can then decide which API to call when loading a stream, either calling the API to return the user's stream, or by calling the search API.

What did we do?

We created and defined our data model for our app. We've defined two objects, `TwitterUser` and `TwitterStream`, and saw how they interact.

Implementing the data model

This section describes the implementation of our data model.

Getting ready

We'll be creating two files, `twitter.js` and `twitterUsers.js`. Place these in the `www/models` directory.

How to do it...

Let's start with the `twitter.js` file:

```
var TWITTER = TWITTER || {};
```

As always, we define our namespace; in this case, `TWITTER`:

```
TWITTER._baseURL = "http://api.twitter.com/1/";
TWITTER._searchBase = "http://search.twitter.com/";
```

We define two variables global to the TWITTER namespace: _baseURL and _searchBase. These two URLs point at Twitter's JSON API; the first is for API requests such as user lookups, user streams, and such, while the latter is only for searching. We define them here for two reasons: to make the URLs a little less nasty in the following code, and if Twitter should ever decide to have a different version of the API (and you want to change it), you can do so here.

Next, we define our first object, TwitterUser using the following code snippet:

```
TWITTER.TwitterUser = function ( theScreenName, completion )
{
    var self = this;
    self._screenName = "";
    self._userData   = {};
```

We've defined our two properties here, _screenName and _userData. We're using underscores at the front to indicate that these are internal (private) variables that no outside object should access. Instead, an outside object should use the get/set methods we define next:

```
self.getScreenName = function ()
{
  return self._screenName;
}
```

This one's simple enough, it just returns the private member when asked. But the next one's more complicated:

```
self.setScreenName = function ( theScreenName, completion
    )
{
    self._screenName = theScreenName;
```

Like a normal set method, we've assigned theScreenName to _screenName. But when this happens, we want to load in the user information from Twitter. This is why it is important to have get/set methods in front of private methods; you might just need them to do something important when the value changes or is read.

```
var getUserURL = TWITTER._baseURL +
    "users/lookup.json?screen_name=" +
    encodeURIComponent(theScreenName);
```

Here we've defined our URL that we're going to use to ask Twitter to look up the user in question. For more information about how this particular URL works, see the Twitter documentation at https://dev.twitter.com/docs/api/1/get/users/lookup. You can see a full example of what is returned at the bottom of the page.

We use the `encodeURIComponent()` method to ensure that the text is properly encoded (so that it can handle international characters).

Now that we have our URL, we're going to use another utility function defined for us in `PKUTIL` (`www/framework/utility.js`), called `loadJSON()`. It uses AJAX to send a request to the earlier URL, and Twitter then sends a response back, in the form of JSON. When it is finished, the function will call the `completion` function we're passing as the second parameter after `getUserURL`. This method can check if the request succeeded or not, and set any private members that are necessary. We'll also call the `completion` function passed to the `setScreenName()` method.

```
PKUTIL.loadJSON ( getUserURL, function (
        success, data )
    {
      if (success)
      {
        self._userData = data;
```

If success is true, then the JSON has been properly returned and parsed into the data parameter. We just assign it to the private `_userData` member.

```
      }
      else
      {
        self._userData = { "error": "Twitter error; rate
            limited?" };
```

But, if the return value of `success` is `false`, then something's gone wrong. Anything could have happened. Twitter might be down (not unheard of), the network connection might have failed, or Twitter might have rate limited us. (For Twitter's error codes, see `https://dev.twitter.com/docs/error-codes-responses`.) For now, we're just going to assume the latter, but you could certainly build more complicated error-detection schemes to figure out the type of error.

```
      }
      if (completion)
      {
          completion ();
      }
```

Finally, regardless of success or failure, we call the `completion` function passed to us. This `completion` function is important so that we know when we can safely access the `_userData` member (via `getUserData` a little lower).

```
      }
    );
  }
```

```
self.getProfileImageURL = function ()
{
    if (self._userData[0])
    {
        return self._userData[0].profile_image_url;
    }
    return "";
}
```

The method `getProfileImageURL()` is a convenience function that returns the user's profile image URL. This is a link to the avatar being used for Twitter. First we check to see if `_userData[0]` exists, and if it does, return `profile_image_url`, a value defined by the Twitter API. If it doesn't, we'll just return an empty string.

```
self.getUserData = function ()
{
    return self._userData;
}
```

Next, the `getUserData()` method is used to return the `_userData` member. If it has been properly loaded, it will have a lot of values in it, all determined by Twitter. If it has failed to load, it'll have an error property in it, and if it hasn't been loaded at all, it'll be empty.

```
self.getTimeline = function ( theMaxCount, completion )
{
    return new TWITTER.TwitterStream ( "@" +
        self._theScreenName, completion, theMaxCount || 25
        );
}
```

The `getTimeline()` method is also a convenience function used to get the timeline for the Twitter user. `theMaxCount` is the maximum number of tweets to return (up to 200), and `completion` is a function to call when it's all done. We do this by creating a new `TwitterStream` object (defined later) with the Twitter screen name prepended by an @ character.

If `theMaxCount` isn't specified, we use a little || trick to indicate the default value of 25 tweets.

```
self.setScreenName ( theScreenName, completion );
}
```

The last thing we do is actually call the `setScreenName()` method with the screen name and `completion` function passed in to the constructor. If you remember your JavaScript, this whole function, while we can think of it as defining an object, is also the constructor of that object. In this case, as soon as you create the `TwitterUser` object, we'll fire off a request to Twitter to load in the user's data and set it to `_userData`.

Our next object is the `TwitterStream` object:

```
TWITTER.TwitterStream = function (
    theScreenNameOrSearchPhrase, completion, theMaxCount )
{
    var self = this;

    self._searchPhrase = "";
    self._stream       = {};
    self._theMaxCount   = 25;
```

Here we've defined three properties, `_searchPhrase`, `_stream`, and `_theMaxCount`. The `_searchPhrase` property can either be the screen name of a user or a literal search term, such as a hashtag. The `_stream` property is the actual collection of tweets obtained from Twitter, and the `_theMaxCount` property is the maximum number of tweets to ask for. (Keep in mind that Twitter is free to return less than this amount.)

You may ask why we're storing either a search phrase or a screen name. The reason is that we're attempting to promote some code re-use. It's logical to assume that a Twitter stream is a Twitter stream, regardless of how it was found, either by asking for a particular user's stream or by searching for a word. Fair assumption, right?

Yeah, but totally wrong, too. The streams are close enough so that we can work around the differences, but still, not the same. So, even though we're treating them here as one-and-the-same, they really aren't – at least until Twitter decides to change their Search API to better match their non-Search API.

```
    self.setMaxCount = function ( theMaxCount )
    {
        self._theMaxCount = theMaxCount;
    }

    self.getMaxCount = function ()
    {
        return self._theMaxCount;
    }
```

Here we have the `get`/`set` methods for the `_theMaxCount` property. All we do is set and retrieve the value. One thing to note is that this should be called before we actually load a stream. This value is part of the ultimate URL we sent to Twitter.

```
    self.setScreenName = function ( theScreenName )
    {
        self._searchPhrase = "@" + theScreenName;
    }

    self.setSearchPhrase = function ( theSearchPhrase )
```

```
{
    self._searchPhrase = theSearchPhrase;
}
self.getSearchPhrase = function ()
{
    return self._searchPhrase;
}
```

Notice that we have two `set` methods that act on the `_searchPhrase` property while we only have one `get` method. What we're doing here is permitting someone to call the `setScreenName()` method without the `@` character. The `_searchPhrase` property will then be set with the `@` character prepended to the screen name. The next `set` method (`setSearchPhrase()`) is intended to be used when setting real search terms (such as a hashtag).

Internally, we'll use the `@` character at the front to mean something special, but you'll see that in a second.

```
self.getStream = function ()
{
    return self._stream;
}
```

The `getStream()` method just returns the `_stream` property, which if we haven't loaded, will be blank. So let's look at the `loadStream()` method:

```
self.loadStream = function ( completion )
{
    var theStreamURL;
    var forScreenName = false;
```

The `loadStream()` method takes a `completion` function. We'll call this at the end of the operation no matter what; it lets the rest of our code know when it is safe to access the `_stream` member via the `getStream()` method.

The other component is the `forScreenName` variable; if `true`, we'll be asking Twitter for the stream that belongs to the screen name stored in the `_searchPhrase` property. Otherwise, we'll ask Twitter to do an actual search for the `_searchPhrase` property:

```
if (self._searchPhrase.substr(0,1)=="@")
{
    theStreamURL = TWITTER._baseURL +
      "statuses/user_timeline.json?include_entities=
       true&include_rts=true&count=" +
       self._theMaxCount + "&screen_name=" +
          encodeURIComponent(self._searchPhrase);
       forScreenName = true;
```

```
    }
    else
    {
        theStreamURL = TWITTER._searchBase +
            "search.json?q=" +
            encodeURIComponent(self._searchPhrase) +
            "&include_entities=true" +
            "&include_rts=true&rpp=" + self._theMaxCount;
        forScreenName = false;
    }
```

All we've done so far is defined the `theStreamURL` property to point either at the Search API (for a search term) or the non-Search API (for a screen name's stream). Next we'll load it with the `loadJSON()` method using the following code snippet:

```
PKUTIL.loadJSON ( theStreamURL, function (success,
    data)
    {
    if (success)
    {
        if (forScreenName)
        {
            self._stream = data;
        }
        else
        {
            self._stream = data.results;
        }
    }
```

Here's another reason why we need to know if we're processing for a screen name or for a search: the JSON we get back is slightly different. When searching, Twitter helpfully includes other information (such as the time it took to execute the search). In our case, we're not interested in anything but the results, hence the two separate code paths.

```
    else
    {
        self._stream = { "error": "Twitter error; rate
            limited?" };
    }
```

Again, if we have a failure, we're assuming that we are rate-limited.

```
    if (completion)
    {
        completion( self._stream );
    }
```

When done, we call the `completion` method, helpfully passing along the data stream.

```
                }
            );
        }
        self.setSearchPhrase ( theScreenNameOrSearchPhrase );
        self.setMaxCount ( theMaxCount || 25 );
        self.loadStream ( completion );
    }
```

Just like at the end of the previous object, we call some methods at the end of this object too. First we set the incoming search phrase, then we set the maximum number of tweets to return (or 25, if it isn't given to us), and then we call the `loadStream()` method with the `completion` function. This means that the moment we create a new `TwitterStream` object, it's already working on loading all the tweets we'll be wanting to have access to.

We've taken care of almost all our data model requirements, but we've got just a little bit left to do in the `twitterUsers.js` file; use the following instruction:

```
TWITTER.users = Array();
```

First, we create a `users()` array in the Twitter namespace. We're going to use this to store our predefined Twitter users, which will be loaded with the following `loadTwitterUsers()` method:

```
TWITTER.loadTwitterUsers = function ( completion )
{
   TWITTER.users.push ( new TWITTER.TwitterUser ( "photoKandy"  ,
function ()
     { TWITTER.users.push ( new TWITTER.TwitterUser ( "CNN"  ,
     function ()
       { TWITTER.users.push ( new TWITTER.TwitterUser (
       "BBCWorld" , function ()
         { TWITTER.users.push ( new TWITTER.TwitterUser (
         "espn", function ()
           { TWITTER.users.push ( new TWITTER.TwitterUser (
           "lemondefr", completion ) ); }
           ) ); }
         ) ) ; }
       ) ) ; }
     ) ) ;
   }
```

What we've done here is essentially just chained together five requests for five different Twitter accounts. You can store these in an array and ask for them all at once. But for this our app needs to know when they've all been loaded. You could also do this by using recursion through an array of users, but we'll leave it as an example to you, the reader.

We have implemented our data model and predefined the five Twitter accounts we want to use. We also went over the `loadJSON()` method in `PKUTIL`, which helps with the entire process. We've also been introduced to the Twitter API.

There's more...

Before we go on, let's take a look at the `loadJSON()` method you've been introduced to. It's been added to this project's `www/framework/utility.js` file, as shown in the following code block:

```
PKUTIL.loadJSON = function ( theURL, completion )
{
    PKUTIL.load( theURL, true, function ( success, data )
        {
```

First off, this is a pretty simple function to begin with. What we're really doing is utilizing the `PKUTIL.load()` method (explained later) to do the hard work of calling out to the URL and passing us the response, but when the response is received, it's going to be coming back to us in the data variable.

```
var theParsedData = {};
```

The `theParsedData` variable will store the actual JSON data, fully parsed.

```
if (success)
{
    try
    {
        theParsedData = JSON.parse ( data );
```

If the URL returns something successfully, we try to parse the data. Assuming it is a valid JSON string, it'll be put into `theParsedData`. If it isn't, the `JSON.parse()` method will throw an exception as follows:

```
    }
    catch (err)
    {
        console.log ("Failed to parse JSON from " + theURL);
        success = COMPLETION_FAILURE;
    }
```

Any exceptions will be logged to the console, and we'll end up telling our completion function that the request failed:

```
}
if (completion)
{
```

```
        completion (success, theParsedData);
    }
```

At the end, we call the `completion` function and tell it if the request failed or succeeded, and what the JSON data was (if successfully parsed).

```
    }
  );
}
```

The `PKUTIL.load()` method is another interesting beast (for full implementation details, visit `https://github.com/photokandyStudios/YASMF/blob/master/framework/utility.js#L126`). It's defined as follows:

```
PKUTIL.load = function ( theFileName, aSync, completion )
{
```

First, we'll check to see if the browser understands `XMLHttpRequest`. If it doesn't, we'll have to call the `completion` function with a failure notice and a message describing how we couldn't load anything. This is shown in the following code block:

```
if (!window.XMLHttpRequest)
{
  if (completion)
  {
    completion ( PKUTIL.COMPLETION_FAILURE,
                 "This browser does not support
                  XMLHttpRequest." );
    return;
  }
}
```

Next we set up the `XMLHttpRequest()` method, and assign the `onreadystatechange` function as shown in the following code snippet:

```
var r = new XMLHttpRequest();
r.onreadystatechange = function()
{
```

This function can be called many times during the loading process, so we check for a specific value. In this case, 4 in the following code snippet means that the content has been loaded:

```
if (r.readyState == 4)
{
```

Of course, just because we got data doesn't mean that it is useable data; we need to verify the status of the load, and here we get into a little bit of murky territory. iOS defines success with a zero value, while Android defines it with 200, as shown in the following code snippet:

```
if ( r.status==200 || r.status == 0)
{
```

If we've successfully loaded the data, we'll call the completion function with a success notification and the data:

```
if (completion)
{
   completion ( PKUTIL.COMPLETION_SUCCESS,
                  r.responseText );
}
}
```

But, if we've failed to load the data, we call the completion function with a failure notification and the status value of the load:

```
else
{
  if (completion)
  {
    completion ( PKUTIL.COMPLETION_FAILURE,
                  r.status );
  }
 }
 }
}
```

Keep in mind that we're still just setting up the XMLHttpRequest object; we've not actually triggered the load yet.

The next step is to specify the path to the file, and here we run into a problem on WP7 versus Android and iOS. On both Android and iOS we can load files relative to the index.html file, but on WP7, we have to load them relative to the /app/www directory. Subtle to track down, but critically important. Even though we aren't supporting WP7 in this book, the framework does, and so it needs to handle cases such as the following:

```
if (device.platform=="WinCE")
{
   r.open ('GET', "/app/www/" + theFileName, aSync);
}
else
{
   r.open ('GET', theFileName, aSync);
}
```

Now that we've set the filename, we fire off the load:

```
r.send ( null );

}
```

Should you ever decide to support WP7, it is critical that even though the framework supports passing `false` for `aSync`, which should result in a synchronous load, you shouldn't actually ever do so. WP7's browser does very funny things when it can't load data asynchronously. For one thing, it loads it asynchronously anyway (not your intended behavior), and it also has a tendency to think the file simply doesn't exist. So, instead of loading scripts, you'll get errors in the console indicating that a 404 error has occurred. And you'll scratch your head (I did!) wondering how in the world that could be when the file is right there. Then you'll remember this tip, change the value back to `true`, and things will suddenly start working. (You seriously do not want to know the hours it took me to debug on WP7 to finally figure this out. I want those hours back!)

Configuring the ChildBrowser plugin

Most PhoneGap plugins aren't terribly hard to install or configure, but they will undoubtedly play a vital role in your app, especially if you need to use a feature that PhoneGap doesn't provide on its own.

In our case, we need only one plugin to display websites within our app using a plugin called ChildBrowser.

Getting ready

If you haven't already, you should download the entire community PhoneGap plugin repository located at `https://github.com/phonegap/phonegap-plugins`. This will provide you nearly all the content necessary to use the plugins.

How to do it...

We're going to split this one up into what we have to do for each platform as the steps and environments are all quite different.

Plugin configuration for iOS

Let's look first at the steps necessary for installing the ChildBrowser plugin:

1. Open the collection of plugins you downloaded and navigate to `iOS/ChildBrowser`.

2. Drag `ChildBrowser.bundle`, `ChildBrowserCommand.h`, `ChildBrowserCommand.m`, `ChildBrowserViewController.h`, `ChildBrowserViewController.m`, and `ChildBrowserViewController.xib` into XCode to the `Socializer/Plugins` folder as shown in the following screenshot:

3. At the prompt, make sure to copy the files (instead of linking to them), as shown in the following screenshot:

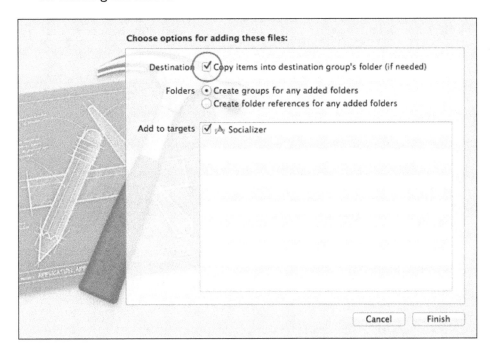

Choose options for adding these files:

Destination ☑ Copy items into destination group's folder (if needed)

Folders ● Create groups for any added folders
○ Create folder references for any added folders

Add to targets ☑ Socializer

Cancel   Finish

4. Copy the `ChildBrowser.js` file to your `www/plugins/iOS` directory. You can do this in XCode or in Finder.

5. Add the plugin to `Cordova.plist` in `Socializer/Supporting Files` in XCode:

   ❑ Find the `Plugins` row, and add a new entry as shown in the following table:

ChildBrowserCommand	String	ChildBrowserCommand

This can be better represented by the following screenshot:

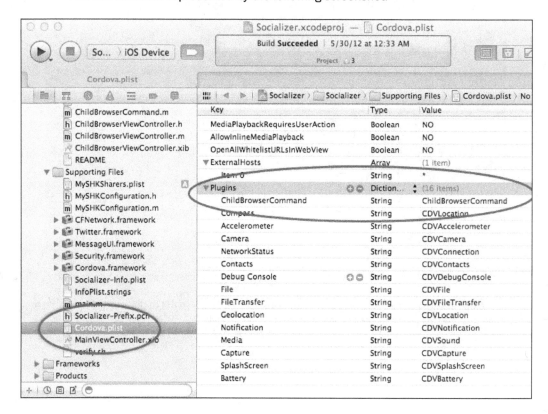

There, that wasn't too bad, right?

6. The final step is to update our `www/index.html` file to include this plugin for our app. Add the following lines after the line that is loading the `"cordova-2.2.0-ios.js"` script:

```
<script type="application/javascript" charset="utf-8"
    src="./plugins/iOS/ChildBrowser.js"></script>
```

Plugin configuration for Android

For Android, we'll be using the same plugin, located in the repository you should have already downloaded from GitHub (although it will be under another directory). Let's start by installing and configuring ChildBrowser using the following steps:

1. Create a new package (**File | New | Package**) under your project's `src` folder. Name it as `com.phonegap.plugins.childBrowser`.

2. Navigate to `Android/ChildBrowser/src/com/phonegap/plugins/childBrowser` and drag the `ChildBrowser.java` file to the newly created package in Eclipse.

3. Go to the `res/xml` folder in your project and open the `config.xml` file with the text editor (usually this is done by a right-click on the file, **Open With | Text Editor**).

4. Add the following line at the bottom of the file, just above the `</plugins>` ending tag:

    ```
    <plugin name="ChildBrowser" value="com.phonegap.plugins.
    childBrowser.ChildBrowser"/>
    ```

5. Navigate to the `Android/ChildBrowser/www` folder in the repository.

6. Copy `childbrowser.js` to `assets/www/plugins/Android`.

7. Copy the `childbrowser` folder to `assets/www`. (Copy the folder, not the contents. You should end up with `assets/www/childbrowser` when done.)

8. The last step is to update our `www/index_Android.html` file by adding the following lines just below the portion that is loading the `cordova-2.0.0-android.js` file:

    ```
    <script type="application/javascript" charset="utf-8" src="./
    plugins/Android/childbrowser.js"></script>
    ```

That's it. Our plugin is correctly installed and configured for Android.

There's more...

We've not actually dealt with *how* to use the plugin we just installed. We'll be dealing with that as we come to the necessary steps when implementing our project. But there is one important detail to pay attention to—the plugin's readme file, if available.

This file will often indicate the installation steps necessary, or any quirks that you might need to watch out for. The proper use of the plugin is also usually detailed. Unfortunately, some plugins don't come with instructions; at that point, the best thing to do is to try installing it in the *normal* fashion (as we've done earlier for the ChildBrowser plugin) and see if it works.

The other thing to remember is that PhoneGap is an ongoing project. This means that there are plugins that are out-of-date (and indeed, some have had to be updated by the author for this book) and won't work correctly with the most recent versions of PhoneGap. You'll need to pay attention to the plugins so that you know which version it supports, and if it needs to be modified to work with a newer version of PhoneGap. Modifications usually aren't terribly difficult, but it does involve getting into the native code, so you may wish to ask the community (located at `http://groups.google.com/group/phonegap`) for any help in the modification.

Implementing the start view

To create our view, we need to create the file for it first. The file should be called `startView.html`, and should live under the `www/views` directory. The view we're creating will end up looking like the following screenshot for iOS:

The view for Android will look like the following screenshot:

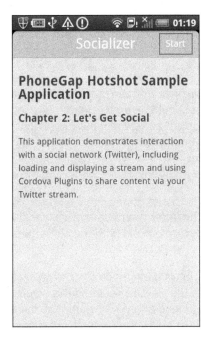

Before we actually create the view though, let's define the structure of our view. Depending upon the framework in use, the structure of a view can be vastly different. For the YASMF framework, our view will consist of some HTML that will depend on some pre-defined CSS, and some JavaScript defined below that same HTML. You could easily make the case that the JavaScript and inline styles should be separated out as well, and if you wish, you can do so.

The HTML portion for all our views will be of the form of the following code block:

```
<div class="viewBackground">
 <div class="navigationBar">
  <div id="theView_AppTitle"></div>
  <button class="barButton backButton"
   id="theView_backButton" style="left:10px" ></button>
</div>
<div class="content avoidNavigationBar avoidToolBar"
  id="theView_anId">
</div>
 <div class="toolBar">
  <button class="barButton" id="theView_aButton"
  style="right:10px"></button>
 </div>
</div>
```

As you can see, there's no visible text anywhere in this code. Since everything must be localized, we'll be inserting the text programmatically via JavaScript.

The `viewBackground` class will be our view's container. Everything related to the view's structure is defined within. The style is defined in `www/framework/base.css` and `www/style/style.css`: the latter is for our app's custom styles.

The `navigationBar` class indicates that the `div` class is just a navigation bar. For iOS users, this has instant meaning, but it should be pretty clear to everyone else. This bar holds the title of the view, as well as any buttons that serve for navigation (such as a **back** button). Notice that the **title** and **back** button both have `id` values. This makes it easy for us to access them in our JavaScript later on. Notice also that we are namespacing these IDs with the view name and an underscore; this is to prevent any issues with using the same `id` twice.

The next `div` class is given the class of `content avoidNavigationBar avoidToolBar`, where all the content will go. The latter two classes specify that it should be offset from the top of the screen and short enough to avoid both the navigation bar (already defined) and the toolbar (coming up).

Finally, the toolbar is defined. This is a bar much like the navigation bar, but is intended to hold buttons that are related to the view. For Android this would be commonly shown near or at the top of the screen, while iPhone and WP7 display this bar at the bottom. (iPad, on the other hand, would display this just below the navigation bar or on the navigation bar.)

Below this HTML block, we'll define any templates we may need for localization, and then finally any JavaScript we need.

How to do it...

With all the discussed points in mind, let's create our start view, which should be named `startView.html` in the `www/views` directory, as shown in the following code block:

```html
<div class="viewBackground">
  <div class="navigationBar">
    <div id="startView_AppTitle"></div>
    <button class="barButton" id="startView_startButton"
    style="right:10px"></button>
  </div>
  <div class="content avoidNavigationBar" id="startView_welcome">
  </div>
</div>
```

This code snippet looks similar like our view template defined earlier except that we're missing a back button and a toolbar. The first is due to the fact that the first view we display to the user doesn't have anything to go back to, so we omit that button. Views don't have to have toolbars, so we're omitting it here. The `id` values have also changed to include the name of our view.

None of this defines what our view will look like, though. To determine that, we need to override our framework styles in `www/framework/base.css` by setting them in `www/style/style.css`.

First, we define the look of the `navigationBar` class, we use the glossy black bar from our template defined earlier in this chapter, as shown in the following code snippet:

```
.navigationBar
{
  background-image: url(../images/NavigationBar.png);
  color: #FFF;
  background-color: transparent;
  border-top-left-radius: 10px;
  border-top-right-radius: 10px;
  z-index:1;
  box-shadow: 0px 3px 10px #888;
}
```

The view's background is defined as follows:

```
.viewBackground
{
  border-radius: 10px;
  background-color: #000;
}
```

The toolbar is defined similar to the navigation bar as follows:

```
.toolBar
{
  background-color: #628799;
}
```

The content area has a textured background, which is defined as follows:

```
.content
{
  background-image: url(../images/Background.png);
  background-repeat: repeat;
  background-size: 50% 50%;
  color: #333;
}
```

There rest of the styling is related to specific items in our app (such as avatars), shown as follows:

```css
.toolBar .profileImage
{
  width: 32px;
  height: 32px;
  display: inline-block;
  line-height: 44px;
  margin-left:10px;
  margin-right:10px;
  background-size: 32px 32px;
  background-repeat: no-repeat;
  margin-top: 6px;
}

.twitterItem
{
  height: auto;
  padding:10px;
  padding-bottom: 20px;
  background-image: -webkit-linear-gradient(top,
  rgba(255,255,255,0.5), rgba(0,0,0,0.25) );
  background-repeat: repeat-y;
  border-bottom: 1px solid #000;
}

.twitterItem img
{
  float: left;
  margin-right:10px;
  margin-bottom: 10px;
}

.twitterName
{
  height: 32px;
  line-height: 32px;
}

.twitterRealName
{
  font-weight: bold;
}
```

```css
.twitterScreenName
{
  color: #888;
}


.twitterTweet
{
  margin-top:10px;
  height: auto;
}


.twitterEntities .entity
{
  height:auto;
  position: relative;
  margin-top:10px;
  border-radius: 10px;
  border: 1px solid #888;
  background-color: rgba(255,255,255,.25);
  padding:10px;
}

.twitterEntities A, .twitterEntities A:visited, .twitterEntities
A:link, .twitterEntities A:hover
{
 text-decoration: none;
}


.twitterEntities A.touched
{
  text-decoration: underline;
  text-shadow: 0px 0px 10px #FFF;
}


.twitterEntities .entity.hash, .twitterEntities .entity.user
{
  display: inline-block;
  margin-right:10px;
}


.twitterEntities .entity.hash A
{
  color: #800 !important;
}
```

```
.twitterEntities .entity.user A
{
  color: #080 !important;
}


.twitterEntities .entity.url
{
  display: block;
}


.twitterEntities .entity.url A
{
  color: #008 !important;
 display: block;
}
```

That's everything needed to make our start view start to look like a real app. Of course, there's a lot of pre-built stuff in `www/framework/base.css`, which you're welcome to analyze and reuse in your own projects.

Now that we've defined the view and the appearance, we need to define some of the view's content. We're going to do this by using a hidden `div` class as shown in the following code snippet:

```
<div id="startView_welcome_en" class="hidden">
    <h2>PhoneGap Hotshot Sample Application</h2>
    <h3>Chapter 2: Let's Get Social</h3>
    <p>This application demonstrates interaction
       with a social network (Twitter), including
       the following items:
    </p>
      <ul>
        <li>Retrieving information about users</li>
        <li>Displaying a specific user's stream</li>
        <li>Searching Twitter for a specific hashtag</li>
        <li>Displaying external webpages in a Child Browser</li>
        <li>Using Twitter Web Intents to share to your followers on
        Twitter</li>
      </ul>
</div>
```

This `div` block is classed as `hidden` so that it won't be visible to the user. We'll then use some JavaScript to copy the content to the content area inside the view.

Next comes the JavaScript shown as follows:

```
<script>

  var startView = $ge("startView") || {};  // properly namespace
```

Our first act is to put all our script into a namespace. Unlike most of our other namespace definitions, we're actually going to piggyback onto the `startView` element (which the astute reader will notice has not been defined yet; that'll be near the end of this chapter). While the element is a proper DOM element, it also serves a perfect place for us to attach to, as long as we avoid any of the cardinal sins of using DOM method names as our own which, I promise, we won't do.

You might be wondering what `$ge` does. Since we're not including any JavaScript framework such as jQuery, we don't have a convenience method to get an element by its ID. jQuery does this with `$()`, and because you might actually be using jQuery along with the framework we're using, I chose to use `$ge()`, short for *get element*. It's defined in `www/framework/utility.js` as shown in the following code snippet. All it does is act as a shortened version of `document.getElementById`.

```
function $ge ( elementId )
{
   return document.getElementById ( elementId );
}
```

Back to our start view script, we define what needs to happen when the view is initialized. Here we hook into the various buttons and other interface elements that are in the view, as well as localize all the text and content as shown in the following code snippet:

```
startView.initializeView = function() {

   startView.applicationTitleImage = $ge("startView_AppTitle");

   startView.applicationTitleImage.innerHTML = __T("APP_TITLE");
```

This is our first use of the `__T()` method. Using this method is how we can properly localize an image or text. Of course, we're using English as the language for this app, but it never hurts to prepare for localization and globalization by building it in from the start. If you want to know more about how the framework supports internationalization, visit `https://github.com/photokandyStudios/YASMF/wiki/PKLOC`. We can localize our start button using the following code lines:

```
   startView.startButton = $ge("startView_startButton");
   startView.startButton.innerHTML = __T("START");
```

Now we've properly localized our start button, but how do we make it do anything? For this we can use a little function defined in www/framework/ui-core.js called PKUI.CORE. addTouchListener() as shown in following code block:

```
PKUI.CORE.addTouchListener(startView.startButton, "touchend",
startView.startApp);
```

Finally we need to display the correct *welcome* text in the content area as follows:

```
var theWelcomeContent = $geLocale("startView_welcome");
$ge("startView_welcome").innerHTML =
theWelcomeContent.innerHTML;

}
```

Next up in our start view script, we have the function that is called whenever the start button is tapped, as seen in the following code block:

```
startView.startApp = function() {
    PKUI.CORE.pushView(socialView);
}


</script>
```

Real short, but packs a punch. This code block displays our social view to the player, which actually starts the app. If you want to know more about how the pushView() method works, visit https://github.com/photokandyStudios/YASMF/wiki/PKUI.CORE.pushView.

Whew! That was a lot of work for a pretty simple view. Thankfully, most of the work is actually done by the framework, so our actual startView.html file is pretty small.

There's more...

It probably doesn't take much to guess, but there's several complementary functions to the pushView() method – popView, showView, and hideView.

The popView function does the exact opposite of pushView. It moves the views right (instead of left) by popping them off the view stack.

The showView and hideView functions do essentially the same thing, but simpler. They don't do any animation at all. Furthermore, since they don't involve any other view on the stack, they are most useful at the beginning of an app when we have to figure out how to display our very first view with no previous view to animate.

If you want to know more about view management, you might want to visit https://github.com/photokandyStudios/YASMF/wiki/Understanding-the-View-Stack-and-View-Management and explore https://github.com/photokandyStudios/YASMF/wiki/PKUI.CORE.

Implementing the social view

The social view is where we will display a Twitter stream.

Getting ready

Go ahead and create the `socialView.html` file now based on ours. Then we'll go over the portions you haven't seen before.

How to do it...

When we're finished with this task, we should have a view that looks like the following screenshot for iOS:

The view for Android will look like the following screenshot:

As with all our views to this point, we're going to start with the HTML portion that describes the actual view as follows:

```html
<div class="viewBackground">
 <div class="navigationBar">
  <div id="socialView_title"></div>
  <button class="barButton backButton"
       id="socialView_backButton" style="left:10px" ></button>
 </div>
 <div class="content avoidNavigationBar avoidToolBar"
     style="padding:0; overflow: scroll;"
     id="socialView_scroller">
  <div id="socialView_contentArea" style="padding: 0;
    height: auto; position: relative;">
  </div>
 </div>
 <div class="toolBar" id="socialView_toolbar" style="text-
       align: center">
 </div>
</div>
```

Generally, nothing is too difficult here. We've added a style to the inner `div` block. This takes away our default `div` styling (from `www/framework/base.css`) and forces the height to fit to the content (instead of to the screen). This means that when we want to scroll, we'll have the whole content to scroll through.

Speaking of scrolling, in a perfect world, we could just rely on `overflow:scroll` to work on all our platforms, but that doesn't always work out well. We can rely on native scrolling in iOS 5, but that has its own share of problems, and rules out any lower platform, and of course, it doesn't work on Android at any version. So for iOS and Android we'll have to use our own implementation for scrolling or use a third party scrolling library such as iScroll 4. In this case, we're using our own implementation, which we'll cover a little later.

First, we need to determine how our toolbar will show its profile images using the following template:

```
<div class="hidden" id="socialView_profileImageIcon">
 <a class="profileImage" style="background-
     image:url(%PROFILE_IMAGE_URL%)"
   href="javascript:socialView.loadStreamFor
     ('@%SCREEN_NAME%');"></a>
</div>
```

Note that we have a little bit of JavaScript that fires when the user touches the image. This is to load the appropriate stream for that image.

Next we need to define what the tweets should look like within our view using the following code snippet:

```
<div class="hidden" id="socialView_twitterTemplate">
 <div class="twitterItem" onclick="socialView.selectTweet(%INDEX%);">
  <img src="%PROFILE_IMAGE_URL%" width=32 height=32 border=0
   />
  <div class="twitterName">
   <span class="twitterRealName">%REAL_NAME%</span>
   <span class="twitterScreenName">@%SCREEN_NAME%</span>
  </div>
  <div class="twitterTweet">%TWEET%</div>
 </div>
</div>
```

In this segment of HTML, we've defined what the rest of a tweet should look like. We've given every `div` and `span` a class so that we can target them in our `style.css` file (located in `www/style`). That is mainly to keep the display of the tweet as separate from the content of the tweet as possible, and to make it easy to change the look of a tweet whenever we want. Go ahead and take a look at the `style.css` file to get a good idea of how they will work to give our tweets some style.

Next up, our code:

```
var socialView = $ge("socialView") || {};
socialView.firstTime = true;
socialView.currentStream = {};
socialView.lastScrollTop = 0;
socialView.myScroll = {};
```

As always, we give ourselves a namespace, in this case `socialView`. We also declare a few properties—`firstTime`, which will track if this is the first time our view is being displayed or not, and `currentStream`, which will hold the current visible stream from Twitter. The `lastScrollTop` property will record the position the user has scrolled to on our current page so we can restore it when they return from looking at an individual tweet, and `myScroll` will hold our actual scroller as seen in the following code block:

```
socialView.initializeView = function ()
{
    PKUTIL.include ( ["./models/twitterStreams.js",
        "./models/twitterStream.js"], function ()
                    {
                        // load our toolbar
                        TWITTER.loadTwitterUsers (
                        socialView.initializeToolbar );
                    }
                );

    socialView.viewTitle = $ge("socialView_title");
    socialView.viewTitle.innerHTML = __T("APP_TITLE");

    socialView.backButton = $ge("socialView_backButton");
    socialView.backButton.innerHTML = __T("BACK");
    PKUI.CORE.addTouchListener(socialView.backButton,
        "touchend", function () { PKUI.CORE.popView(); });

    if (device.platform != "WinCE")
    {
        socialView.myScroll = new SCROLLER.
            GenericScroller ('socialView_contentArea');
    }

}
```

Our `initializeView()` method isn't terribly complicated. We've highlighted a couple of lines in the code snippet. However, note that we load our models and when they are complete, we call the `TWITTER.loadTwitterUsers()` method. We pass along a `completion` function, which we define next so that when Twitter has returned the user data for all five of our Twitter users, we can call it.

We've also defined our scroller; if you want to see the complete code take a look in `www/framework/scroller.js`, but suffice it to say, it is a reasonably nice scroller that is simple to use. It doesn't beat native scrolling, but nothing will. You're free to replace it with any library you'd like, but for the purposes of this project, we've gone this route.

```
socialView.initializeToolbar = function ()
{

    var toolbarHtml = "";
    var profileImageTemplate =
        $ge("socialView_profileImageIcon").innerHTML;
    var users = TWITTER.users;

    if (users.error)
    {
        console.log (streams.error);
        alert ("Rate limited. Please try again later.");
    }
```

One of the first things we do after obtaining the template's HTML is to check on our `TWITTER.users` array. This array should have been filled with all sorts of user data, but if Twitter has rate-limited us for some reason, it may not be. So we check to see if there is an error condition, and if so, we let the user know. Granted, it's not the best method to let a user know, but for our example app, it suffices.

```
    // go through each stream and request the profile image
    for (var i=0; i<users.length; i++)
    {
        var theTemplate = profileImageTemplate.replace
            ("%SCREEN_NAME%", users[i].getScreenName())
                        .replace ("%PROFILE_IMAGE_URL%",
                            users[i].getProfileImageURL());
        toolbarHtml += theTemplate;
    }
```

Next, we iterate through each of the users. There should be five users, but you could configure it for a different number and build up an HTML string that we'll put into the toolbar as follows:

```
    $ge("socialView_toolbar").innerHTML = toolbarHtml;
}
```

Our next function, `loadStreamFor()` does the real hard work in this view. It requests a stream from Twitter and then processes it for display; this can be seen in the following code block:

```
socialView.loadStreamFor = function ( searchPhrase )
{
  var aStream = new TWITTER.TwitterStream ( searchPhrase,
  function ( theStream )
    {
```

Something that we need to note here is that we are now inside the `completion` function – the function that will be called when the Twitter stream is obtained.

```
var theTweetTemplate =
    $ge("socialView_twitterTemplate").innerHTML;
var theContentArea = $ge("socialView_contentArea");
var theStreamHTML = "";


if (theStream.error)
{
    console.log (theStream.error);
    alert ("Rate limited. Please try again later.");
}
```

Because Twitter may rate-limit us at any time, we check again for any error in the stream.

```
for (var i=0; i<theStream.length; i++)
{
  var theTweet = theStream[i];
  var theTemplate =
      theTweetTemplate.replace("%INDEX%", i)
                      .replace ("%PROFILE_IMAGE_URL%",
                      theTweet.profile_image_url ||
                      theTweet.user.profile_image_url)
                      .replace ("%REAL_NAME%",
                      theTweet.from_user ||
                      theTweet.user.name)
                      .replace ("%SCREEN_NAME%",
                      theTweet.from_user ||
                      theTweet.user.screen_name)
                      .replace ("%TWEET%",
                      theTweet.text);
      theStreamHTML += theTemplate;
}
```

Here we're iterating through each item in the stream and building up a large HTML string from the template we defined earlier.

One important thing to notice is how we're obtaining the data of the tweet using `theTweet.from_user || theTweet.user.screen_name`. This is to deal with how Twitter returns a slightly different data format when searching for a word or a hashtag versus the data format when returning a user's timeline. Should one of them be undefined, we'll be loading the other, and since we can only get one of them, it's easier than building a lot of `if` statements to take care of it.

```
theContentArea.innerHTML = theStreamHTML;
socialView.currentStream = theStream;
if (socialView.myScroll.scrollTo)
{
    socialView.myScroll.scrollTo ( 0, 0 );
}
```

Once our stream HTML is built, we assign it to the content area so that the user can see it. We also store the stream into the `currentStream` property so that we can reference it later. When that's done, we scroll to the top of the page so that the user can see the most recent tweets.

```
}
        , 100
    );
}
```

You may wonder, what is that last `100`? Well, it's actually a part of the call to the `TwitterStream()` method. It's the number of items to return in the stream.

Our next function deals with what should happen when a user taps on a displayed tweet:

```
socialView.selectTweet = function ( theIndex )
{
    var theTweet = socialView.currentStream[theIndex];
    tweetView.setTweet ( theTweet );
    PKUI.CORE.pushView ( tweetView );
}
```

This function is pretty simple – all we do is tell the tweet view what tweet was tapped, and then push it on to the view stack.

```
socialView.viewWillAppear = function ()
{
    document.addEventListener("backbutton",
        socialView.backButtonPressed, false );
    if (socialView.firstTime)
```

```
            {
                socialView.loadStreamFor ( "@photokandy" );
                socialView.firstTime = false;
            }
            if (socialView.myScroll.scrollTo)
            {
                PKUTIL.delay ( 50, function ()
                    {
                        socialView.myScroll.scrollTo ( 0,
                            socialView.lastScrollTop );
                    }
                );
            }
        }
```

In the `viewWillAppear()` method we're checking if this is the first time the view has been displayed. If it is, we want to load a default stream for the user. Remember, until now we've only loaded a stream when the user taps on a profile image in the toolbar. But we don't want to reload this stream every time our view displays. We could be coming back from the tweet view and the user might want to continue where they left off in the previous stream. In the final portion, we're checking to see if we had a previous scroll position, and if so, we scroll the view to that point. We have to make a delay here since if we set it too early, the view will be offscreen (and won't scroll), or it will be onscreen, and it'll be noticeable to the user.

The remaining two functions, `viewWillHide()` and `backButtonPressed()` are pretty simple, so while you do need them in your code, we won't go over them here.

That's it! Not terribly difficult, but it does what we need. It displays a list of tweets. Once a user taps on the tweet, they'll be taken to the tweet view to do more, and that's what we'll look at in the next task.

In this task, we defined the HTML code and templates for our social view. We also used the Twitter stream data to construct a Twitter stream that the end user can interact with.

Implementing the tweet view

Our tweet view will be where the user interacts with a given tweet. They can open any links within the tweet using the ChildBrowser plugin, or they can search any hashtags contained within the tweet (or any mentions, too). The view also gives the user the opportunity to share the tweet via Twitter Web Intents.

Getting ready

Go ahead and create your `www/tweetView.html` file based on ours. We'll go over the code that is new, while leaving the rest for you to review.

How to do it...

For this next task, we should end up with a view that looks like the following screenshot on an iOS:

The view for Android will look like the following screenshot:

This time, we're not going to display the HTML for defining the layout of our view. You may ask why? This is because you've seen it several times before and can look it up in the code for this project. We're going to start with the templates that will define the content instead:

```
<div class="hidden" id="tweetView_tweetTemplate">
 <div class="twitterItem" onclick="tweetView.selectTweet(%INDEX%);">
  <img src="%PROFILE_IMAGE_URL%" width=64 height=64
   border=0 />
  <div class="twitterRealName">%REAL_NAME%</div>
  <div class="twitterScreenName">@%SCREEN_NAME%</div>
  <div class="twitterTweet">%TWEET%</div>
  <div class="twitterEntities">%ENTITIES%</div>
 </div>
</div>
```

This code is pretty similar to the template in the previous view with a couple of exceptions. One exception is that we've made the profile image larger, and the second is that we've added a `div` class that lists all the *entities* in the tweet. Twitter defines an entity as a URL, a hashtag, or a mention of another twitter user. We'll display any of these that are in a tweet so that the user can tap on them to get more information.

The following code snippet shows our template for any entity. Notice that we've given it the class of `entity` so that all our entities can have a similar appearance:

```
<div class="hidden" id="tweetView_entityTemplate">
  <DIV class="entity %TYPE%">%ENTITY%</DIV>
</div>
```

Next up, we define what each particular entity looks like; in this case, the URL template as seen in the following code snippet:

```
<div class="hidden" id="tweetView_urlEntityTemplate">
 <a href="javascript:PKUTIL.showURL('%URL%');"
   class="openInNewWindow url" target="_blank">%DISPLAYURL%</a>
</div>
```

Note the use of `PKUTIL.showURL()` in this template. This is a convenience method we've defined in PKUTIL to use ChildBrowser to show a webpage. We've done the work of combining how it works on each platform and put it into one function so that it is easy to call. We'll take a look at it a little later.

Refer to the following code block:

```
<div class="hidden" id="tweetView_hashEntityTemplate">
 <a href="javascript:socialView.loadStreamFor('%23%HASHTAG%');
   PKUI.CORE.popView();" class="hash">#%TEXT%</a>
</div>
```

This template is for a hashtag. The big difference between this and the previous template is that it is actually referring back to our previous view! It does this to tell it to load a stream for the hashtag, and then we call the `popView()` method to go back to the view. Chances are the view won't have loaded the information from Twitter just yet, but give it a second and it'll reload with the new stream.

Similarly, the code for a mention is as follows:

```
<div class="hidden" id="tweetView_userEntityTemplate">
 <a href="javascript:socialView.loadStreamFor('@%USER%');
   PKUI.CORE.popView();" class="user" >@%TEXT%</a>
</div>
```

So that defines how our tweet looks and works; let's see how the view actually creates the tweet itself:

```
var tweetView = $ge("tweetView") || {};
tweetView.theTweet = {};
tweetView.setTweet = function ( aTweet )
{
    tweetView.theTweet = aTweet;
}
```

Here, we've defined the `setTweet()` method which stores a given tweet into our `theTweet` property. Remember, this is called from the Twitter stream view when a tweet is tapped to send us the tweet to display.

The next method of interest is `loadTweet()`. We'll skip the `initializeView()` method as it is similar to the previous view. The `loadTweet()` method can be seen in the following code block:

```
tweetView.loadTweet = function ()
{
  var theTweet = tweetView.theTweet;

  var theTweetTemplate =
      $ge("tweetView_tweetTemplate").innerHTML;
  var theEntityTemplate =
      $ge("tweetView_entityTemplate").innerHTML;
  var theURLEntityTemplate =
      $ge("tweetView_urlEntityTemplate").innerHTML;
  var theHashEntityTemplate =
      $ge("tweetView_hashEntityTemplate").innerHTML;
  var theUserEntityTemplate =
      $ge("tweetView_userEntityTemplate").innerHTML;
```

First, we obtain the HTML for each template we need – and there are several!

```
  var theContentArea = $ge("tweetView_contentArea");
  var theTweetHTML = "";
  var theEntitiesHTML = "";

  var theURLEntities = theTweet.entities.urls;
  for (var i=0;i<theURLEntities.length;i++)
  {
      var theURLEntity = theURLEntities[i];
      theEntitiesHTML += theEntityTemplate.replace
                              ("%TYPE%", "url")
                              .replace ("%ENTITY%",
          theURLEntityTemplate.replace ("%URL%",
                              theURLEntity.url )
                              .replace ("%DISPLAYURL%",
                              theURLEntity.display_url )
                          );
  }
```

In this code, we've gone through every URL entity that Twitter has sent us and added it to our entity HTML string. We'll repeat that for hashtags and for mentions, but the code is so similar that we won't repeat it here.

```
var theTemplate = theTweetTemplate
                  .replace ("%PROFILE_IMAGE_URL%",
                  theTweet.profile_image_url ||
                  theTweet.user.profile_image_url)
                  .replace ("%REAL_NAME%",
                  theTweet.from_user ||
                  theTweet.user.name)
                  .replace ("%SCREEN_NAME%",
                  theTweet.from_user ||
                  theTweet.user.screen_name)
                  .replace ("%TWEET%", theTweet.text)
                  .replace ("%ENTITIES%", theEntitiesHTML );
theTweetHTML += theTemplate;
theContentArea.innerHTML = theTweetHTML;
```

Once we've gone through all the entities, we handle the tweet itself. Note that we had to handle the entities first because we handled the substitution earlier. Just like the previous view, we correctly handle the tweet if it is from a search or from a timeline as well.

The next method of interest is the `share()` method, so we'll skip over the `viewWillAppear()`, `viewWillHide()`, and `backButtonPressed()` methods. It should suffice to say, the only different thing the `viewWIllAppear()` method does than any of the others is call the `loadTweet()` method to display the tweet when our view is shown.

The `share()` method is where we call Twitter's Web Intents, as shown in the following code snippet:

```
tweetView.share = function() {
  PKUTIL.showURL("https://twitter.com/intent/tweet?text=" +
encodeURIComponent(tweetView.theTweet.text) + "%20(via%20" +
encodeURIComponent("@" + (tweetView.theTweet.from_user || tweetView.
theTweet.user.screen_name)) + ")");
}
```

Remember that the `showURL()` method is a convenience method to open the ChildBrowser plugin with a specific URL. The URL we are creating has the following components:

- `https://twitter.com/intent/tweet`
- `?text=`
- Encoded `tweetView.theTweet.text`
- `" ( via"`
- `"@"` combined with the screen name who generated the tweet
- `")"`

The idea here is to generate a tweet that looks something like the following:

A tweet that I'm going to tweet to my followers (via @someone)

When added together, the user will be able to go through the following flow to tweet anything they want:

First, if they aren't already logged in to Twitter, they'll be asked to do so, as in the following screenshot:

Next, they'll be presented with the tweet they selected, and will be provided with the opportunity to change it if they want, as in this next screenshot:

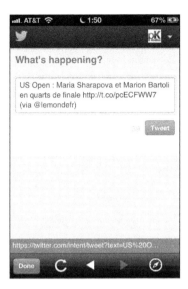

After the tweet has been sent, they will see the following screen:

We displayed a single tweet and processed the various entities within it. We demonstrated loading an external site in the ChildBrowser plugin by using `PKUTIL.showURL()`. We also demonstrated how to use the Twitter Web Intents to share a tweet.

There's more...

Let's take a quick look at `PKUTIL.showURL()`; this method is used to display a ChildBrowser plugin with an external site. It's a pretty simple function, but since it takes three different ways to show the ChildBrowser plugin, we packaged it up into a function that makes it easy to use, as seen in the following code block:

```
PKUTIL.showURL = function ( theURL )
{
    switch (device.platform)
    {
case "Android":
        window.plugins.childBrowser.showWebPage( theURL );
        break;
```

For Android, it's simple to call ChildBrowser. Typically the following code snippet shows how you can call any plugin you want to use in PhoneGap:

```
default:
        cordova.exec("ChildBrowserCommand.showWebPage",
            theURL);
    }
}
```

And for iOS, it's very similar to Android's method, except we call it directly instead of using `window.plugins.childBrowser.showWebPage`.

Well, you've done it! You've successfully written an app that displays information obtained from Twitter and that lets the user share it on Twitter. We also installed a plugin for the first time, and chances are pretty good that you'll need at least the ChildBrowser plugin in nearly every project you do. Thankfully it's also an easy plugin to install!

Putting it all together

We've almost got a fully functional app on our hands, but we're missing a couple of critical components – the parts that load it all and start it off. For this, we'll be creating an `app.js` file and two HTML files under the www directory.

How to do it...

The `index.html` and `index_android.html` files are what kicks everything off by loading the necessary scripts and calling `app.js`.

First, `index.html`, which is intended for iOS is as follows:

```
<!DOCTYPE html>
<html>
  <head>
    <title>Socializer</title>
    <meta name="apple-mobile-web-app-capable" content="yes" />
    <meta name="viewport" content="width=device-width, maximum-
    scale=1.0" />
    <meta name="format-detection" content="telephone=no" />
    <link rel="stylesheet" href="./framework/base.css"
    type="text/css" />
    <link rel="stylesheet" href="./style/style.css"
    type="text/css" />
    <script type="application/javascript" charset="utf-8"
    src="./cordova/cordova-2.2.0-ios.js"></script>
    <script type="application/javascript" charset="utf-8"
    src="./plugins/iOS/ChildBrowser.js"></script>
    <script type="application/javascript" charset="utf-8"
    src="./framework/scroller.js"></script>
    <script type="application/javascript" charset="utf-8"
    src="./framework/utility.js"></script>
    <script type="application/javascript" charset="utf-8"
    src="./app.js"></script>
  </head>
  <body>
    <div class="container" id="rootContainer">
    </div>
    <div id="preventClicks"></div>
  </body>
</html>
```

Next, `index_android.html`, which is for Android is as follows:

```
<!DOCTYPE html>
<html>
  <head>
    <title>Socializer</title>
    <meta name="apple-mobile-web-app-capable" content="yes" />
    <meta name="viewport" content="width=device-width, maximum-
    scale=1.0, target-densityDpi=160" />
    <meta name="format-detection" content="telephone=no" />
    <link rel="stylesheet" href="./framework/base.css"
    type="text/css" />
    <link rel="stylesheet" href="./style/style.css"
    type="text/css" />
```

```
    <script type="application/javascript" charset="utf-8"
    src="./cordova/cordova-2.2.0-android.js"></script>
    <script type="application/javascript" charset="utf-8"
    src="./plugins/Android/childbrowser.js"></script>
    <script type="application/javascript" charset="utf-8"
    src="./framework/scroller.js"></script>
    <script type="application/javascript" charset="utf-8"
    src="./framework/utility.js"></script>
    <script type="application/javascript" charset="utf-8"
    src="./app.js"></script>
  </head>
  <body>
    <div class="container" id="rootContainer">
    </div>
    <div id="preventClicks"></div>
  </body>
</html>
```

The `app.js` file is what actually starts our app. It is also what initializes our localization, sets our current locale, loads various libraries (like `ui-core.js`), and finally, starts our app. Let's look at the code now:

```
var APP = APP || {};
```

As usual, we set up our namespace – this time as `APP`. Next, we'll attach an event listener to the `deviceready` event. This event fires whenever Cordova has finished loading its libraries. We must wait for this event before we can do much of anything, especially anything that relies on Cordova. If we don't, we'll get errors.

```
document.addEventListener("deviceready", onDeviceReady, false);

function onDeviceReady()
{
  APP.start();
}
```

All the function in this code snippet does is call the `APP.start()` method, which is defined as follows:

```
APP.start = function ()
{
  PKUTIL.include ( [ "./framework/ui-core.js",
                     "./framework/device.js",
                     "./framework/localization.js" ],
          function () { APP.initLocalization(); } );
}
```

You've already seen `PKUTIL.include`, so it isn't anything new to you, but here we're loading three libraries, and including a `completion` function to call `APP.initLocalization`. Because the `include` command is asynchronous, we cannot continue writing code after this call that relies on those libraries, or there's a good chance the library wouldn't be loaded in time. Therefore, we call the `initLocalization` function when all three libraries are fully loaded.

The next function, `initLocalization`, initializes all the localization libraries and when complete, we can load any locales we might need. When those locales are finished loading, we call the `APP.init` function and this is where the real work begins.

```
APP.initLocalization = function ()
{
  PKLOC.initializeGlobalization(
   function ()
   {
      PKLOC.loadLocales ( ["en-US"],
      function ()
      {
        APP.init();
      } );
   }
  );
}
```

The `APP.init()` function defines our app's basic translation matrix (you may see translations you've seen before - that's because they originated from here!), and we also proceed to load the three views we have created into the document using the following code snippet:

```
APP.init = function ()
{
```

Next, we have our basic translation matrix: application titles, start, back, and share, as seen in the following code block:

```
PKLOC.addTranslation("en", "APP_TITLE", "Socializer");
PKLOC.addTranslation("en", "START", "Start");
PKLOC.addTranslation("en", "BACK", "Back");
PKLOC.addTranslation("en", "SHARE", "Share");
```

Next, we call a function in `PKUI.CORE` called `initializeApplication`. All this application does is attach a special event handler that tracks the orientation of the device. But by doing so, it also attaches the device, the form factor, and the orientation to the `BODY` element, which is what permits us to target various platforms with CSS.

```
PKUI.CORE.initializeApplication ( );
```

Next, we load a view – `gameView` in this case (order doesn't really matter here):

```
PKUTIL.loadHTML("./views/socialView.html", {
    id: "socialView",
    className: "container",
    attachTo: $ge("rootContainer"),
    aSync: true
}, function(success) {
    if (success) {
      socialView.initializeView();
    }
});
```

We call `PKUTIL.loadHTML` to accomplish this, and if you're thinking it would be a lot like `PKUTIL.include`, you'd be right. We'll look at the definition a little later, but it should suffice to say that, we're loading the content inside `socialView.html`, wrapping it with another `div` with an ID of `socialView` and a class of `container`, attaching it to the `rootContainer`, and indicating that it can be loaded asynchronously.

Once it finishes loading, we'll call the `initializeView()` method on it.

We load the tweet view in the same way as follows:

```
PKUTIL.loadHTML("./views/tweetView.html", {
    id: "tweetView",
    className: "container",
    attachTo: $ge("rootContainer"),
    aSync: true
}, function(success) {
    if (success) {
      tweetView.initializeView();
    }
});
```

We load the start view almost exactly the same way as all the others. I'll highlight the difference in the following code block:

```
PKUTIL.loadHTML ( "./views/startView.html",
                 { id : "startView",
                   className: "container",
                   attachTo: $ge("rootContainer"),
                   aSync: true
                 },
                 function (success)
                 {
                   if (success)
                   {
```

```
                    startView.initializeView();
                    PKUI.CORE.showView (startView);
                }
            });

    }
```

The only thing we do differently is to show the `startView` function after we initialize it. At this point the app is fully loaded and running, and is waiting for the user to tap the **Start** button.

There's More...

Let's look at `PKUTIL.loadHTML` a little closer:

```
PKUTIL.loadHTML = function( theFileName, options, completion )
{
    var aSync = options["aSync"];
```

The first thing we do is pull out the `aSync` option – we need it to call `PKUTIL.load`. Again, the warning about WP7 and loading synchronously still applies; it is best to assume you'll always be using `true` unless you can rule WP7 out of your supported platforms.

```
PKUTIL.load ( theFileName, aSync, function ( success, data )
{
    if (success)
    {
```

At this point, we've successfully loaded the HTML file; now we have to figure out what to do with it.

```
        var theId = options["id"];
        var theClass = options["className"];
        var attachTo = options["attachTo"];
```

First, we extract out the other parameters we need: `id`, `className`, and `attachTo`.

```
        var theElement = document.createElement ("DIV");
        theElement.setAttribute ("id", theId);
        theElement.setAttribute ("class", theClass);
        theElement.style.display = "none";
        theElement.innerHTML = data;
```

Next we create a `DIV` element, and give it the `id` and `class` values. We also load the data into the element.

```
        if (attachTo)
        {
            attachTo.appendChild (theElement);
```

```
   }
   else
   {
      document.body.appendChild (theElement);
   }
```

If possible, we'll attach to the element specified in `attachTo`, but if it isn't defined, we'll attach to the `BODY` element. It is at this point that our element become, a real DOM element in the display hierarchy.

Unfortunately this isn't all! Remember that our HTML files have `SCRIPT` tags in them. For whatever reason, these scripts don't execute automatically when loaded in this fashion; we have to create `SCRIPT` tags for them again as shown in the following code block:

```
var theScriptTags = theElement.getElementsByTagName
      ("script");
```

First, we get all the `SCRIPT` tags in our newly created element. Then we'll iterate through each one, as follows:

```
for (var i=0;i<theScriptTags.length;i++)
{
   try
   {
      // inspired by
      http://bytes.com/topic/javascript/answers/513633-
      innerhtml-script-tag
      var theScriptElement =
            document.createElement("script");
      theScriptElement.type = "text/javascript";
      theScriptElement.charset = "utf-8";
      if (theScriptTags[i].src)
      {
         theScriptElement.src = theScriptTags[i].src;
      }
      else
      {
         theScriptElement.text = theScriptTags[i].text;
      }
      document.body.appendChild (theScriptElement);
```

If this code looks somewhat familiar, it's because it is. `PKUTIL.include` has a variant of it. The important distinction is that it was only concerned about the data of the script – here we have to worry about whether the script is defined as an external script. That's why we check to see if the `SRC` attribute is defined.

We have also surrounded this in a `try-catch` block, just in case the scripts have errors in them:

```
        }
        catch ( err )
        {
          console.log ( "When loading " + theFileName +
                       ", error: " + err );
        }
      }
```

When we've finished loading the HTML and the scripts, call the `completion` function:

```
      if (completion)
      {
        completion (PKUTIL.COMPLETION_SUCCESS);
      }
    }
```

If, for whatever reason, we couldn't load the view, we generate a log message and call the `completion` function with a `failure` notification as follows:

```
      else
      {
        console.log ("WARNING: Failed to load " + theFileName );
        if (completion)
        {
          completion (PKUTIL.COMPLETION_FAILURE);
        }
      }
    }
  );
}
```

As a project, Socializer does what it set out to do, but there's actually so much more that you could do to it to make it truly useful. Why don't you try one or more of the following challenges:

► Instead of using Twitter Web Intents, use the native sharing methods. For iOS, this would likely mean using the ShareKitPlugin. For Android, this probably means using the Share plugin. While the latter plugin isn't too hard to install, I'll warn you now that the ShareKitPlugin for iOS is not easy to install.

► Let the end user select their own initial Twitter accounts, instead of our initial five.

► Display a loading graphic while the Twitter stream is loading so that the user knows that the app is working on something.

- Style any links, mentions, or hashtags in the Twitter stream to make them stand out more.

- Add code to intercept the success page when a tweet is sent. Use this to close the ChildBrowser automatically, rather than requiring the user to intuit that they need to do it for themselves.

- Try your hand at working with the API of any other social network of your choice.

There are some resources that you might find interesting. You might want to look through the YASMF documentation to learn more about the framework we're using. Some of these resources are mentioned as follows:

- Adobe Photoshop at `http://www.adobe.com/PhotoshopFamily`

- GIMP at `http://www.gimp.org`

- PhoneGap downloads at `http://www.phonegap.com/download`

- PhoneGap documentation at `http://docs.phonegap.com`

- YASMF GitHub at `https://github.com/photokandyStudios/YASMF/`

- YASMF documentation at `https://github.com/photokandyStudios/YASMF/wiki/`

- Xcode at `https://developer.apple.com/xcode`

- Eclipse Classic 4.2.1 at `http://www.eclipse.org/downloads/packages/eclipse-classic-421/junosr1`

- Android SDK download at `http://developer.android.com/sdk/index.html`

Thank you for buying
Instant Phonegap Social App Development

About Packt Publishing

Packt, pronounced 'packed', published its first book "*Mastering phpMyAdmin for Effective MySQL Management*" in April 2004 and subsequently continued to specialize in publishing highly focused books on specific technologies and solutions.

Our books and publications share the experiences of your fellow IT professionals in adapting and customizing today's systems, applications, and frameworks. Our solution based books give you the knowledge and power to customize the software and technologies you're using to get the job done. Packt books are more specific and less general than the IT books you have seen in the past. Our unique business model allows us to bring you more focused information, giving you more of what you need to know, and less of what you don't.

Packt is a modern, yet unique publishing company, which focuses on producing quality, cutting-edge books for communities of developers, administrators, and newbies alike. For more information, please visit our website: www.packtpub.com.

Writing for Packt

We welcome all inquiries from people who are interested in authoring. Book proposals should be sent to author@packtpub.com. If your book idea is still at an early stage and you would like to discuss it first before writing a formal book proposal, contact us; one of our commissioning editors will get in touch with you.

We're not just looking for published authors; if you have strong technical skills but no writing experience, our experienced editors can help you develop a writing career, or simply get some additional reward for your expertise.

PhoneGap Beginner's Guide

ISBN: 978-1-84951-536-8   Paperback: 328 pages

Build cross-platform mobile applications with the PhoneGap open source development framework

1. Learn how to use the PhoneGap mobile application framework

2. Develop cross-platform code for iOS, Android, BlackBerry, and more

3. Write robust and extensible JavaScript code

4. Master new HTML5 and CSS3 APIs

PhoneGap Mobile Application Development Cookbook

ISBN: 978-1-84951-858-1   Paperback: 320 pages

Over 40 recipes to create mobile applications using the PhoneGap API with examples and clear instructions

1. Use the PhoneGap API to create native mobile applications that work on a wide range of mobile devices

2. Discover the native device features and functions you can access and include within your applications

3. Packed with clear and concise examples to show you how to easily build native mobile applications

Please check **www.PacktPub.com** for information on our titles

WordPress Mobile Applications with PhoneGap

ISBN: 978-1-84951-986-1   Paperback: 96 pages

A straightforward, example-based guide to leveraging your web development skills to build mobile applications using WordPress, jQuery, jQuery Mobile, and PhoneGap

1. Discover how we can leverage on Wordpress as a content management system and serve content to mobile apps by exposing its API

2. Learn how to build geolocation mobile applications using Wordpress and PhoneGap

3. Step-by-step instructions on how you can make use of jQuery and jQuery mobile to provide an interface between Wordpress and your PhoneGap app

PhoneGap 2 Mobile Application Development Hotshot: RAW

ISBN: 978-1-84951-940-3   Paperback: 350 pages

Create exciting apps for mobile devices using PhoneGap

1. Ten apps included to help you get started on your very own exciting mobile app

2. These apps include working with localization, social networks, geolocation, as well as the camera, audio, video, plugins, and more

3. Apps cover the spectrum from productivity apps, educational apps, all the way to entertainment and games

Please check **www.PacktPub.com** for information on our titles